POTATO

Words that look like **this** can be found in the glossary on page 24.

BookLife
PUBLISHING

©2021
BookLife Publishing Ltd.
King's Lynn
Norfolk PE30 4LS

All rights reserved.
Printed in Malaysia.

A catalogue record for this
book is available from the
British Library.

ISBN: 978-1-83927-159-5

Written by:
Kirsty Holmes

Edited by:
Shalini Vallepur

Designed by:
Dan Scase

CONTENTS

WHAT IS A LIFE CYCLE?

All animals, plants and humans go through different stages of their life as they grow and change. This is called a life cycle.

Human life cycle

Baby → Child → Adult

WHAT IS A POTATO?

A potato is a type of plant. A plant is a living thing that can make its own food from water and sunlight. The potato is a type of **edible** plant.

Flowers

Stem

Roots

Leaves

Farmers grow potatoes for us to eat as food.

SEEDS

The potato plant makes seeds. Potato seeds are found inside the potato berry. This is a small green fruit.

Potato berries

Never eat the berries if you see them! They are very poisonous.

Potato plants that grow from seeds have been **pollinated** by a different potato plant.

How do we get the same tasty potato every time?

TUBERS

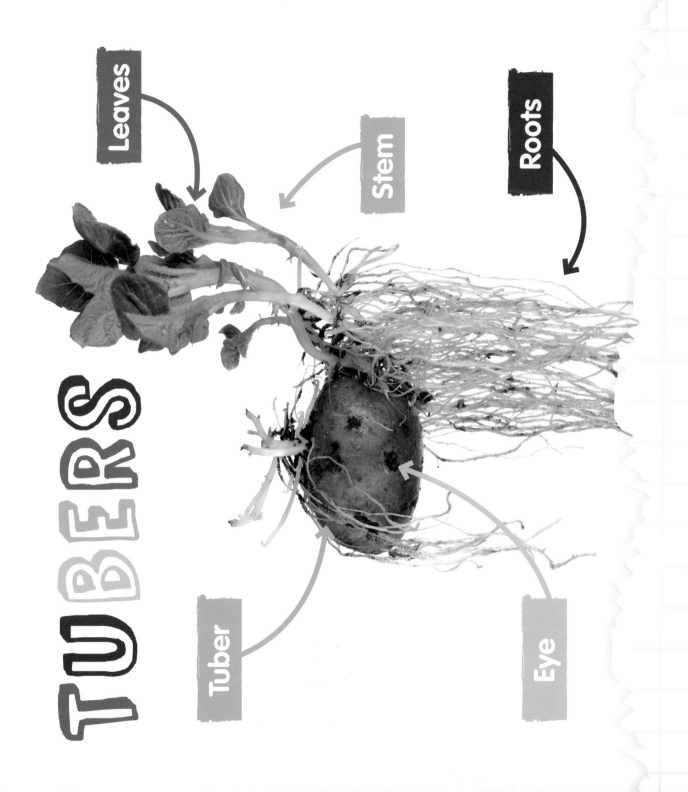

Leaves

Stem

Roots

Tuber

Eye

New potato plants can be grown from the potato. This is called cloning. The potato itself is a part of the plant called a tuber.

A tuber is a stem that grows below the ground and stores **nutrients**. Potatoes have small, dark buds on them that look like hard spots. These are called eyes – but they're not for seeing!

Potato or tuber

Eye

A new plant can grow from the eye of the potato.

New plant or sprout

PLANTING

Before being planted in soil, **<u>chitting</u>** can take place. Sprouts grow from the potato eyes. After chitting, the sprouted tuber can be planted. Planted tubers need soil and water to grow, but not light.

Sprout

Potatoes like damp soil. If the soil dries out, sunlight could get on the potato and turn it green. The green part of the potato can also be poisonous, like the berries.

Don't eat the green parts – you can cut them off and throw them away.

LEAVES AND ROOTS

The potato shoot will grow towards the surface, and leaves will begin to grow above the soil. The leaves will take in **energy** from the Sun and turn it into food for the plant.

Potato plant leaves are lush and green.

The plant also grows roots. Roots are not the same thing as tubers. The roots take in nutrients from the ground. These nutrients are then stored in the tubers.

FLOWERS AND FRUIT

When the plant is ready, it will grow flowers. Potato flowers are small and shaped like stars. They are often white, pink or purple.

Flower

If the flowers are pollinated, they grow into fruit. The fruit will fall to the ground and **rot** away. The seeds inside this fruit can now grow into a new plant.

If the potato flower isn't pollinated, or if the plant doesn't flower at all, it will grow again from the tubers buried in the soil.

POTATOES

Once the plant has flowered, tubers will form at the tips of some roots. The plant starts to fill up the tubers with water and nutrients. They get bigger as they fill.

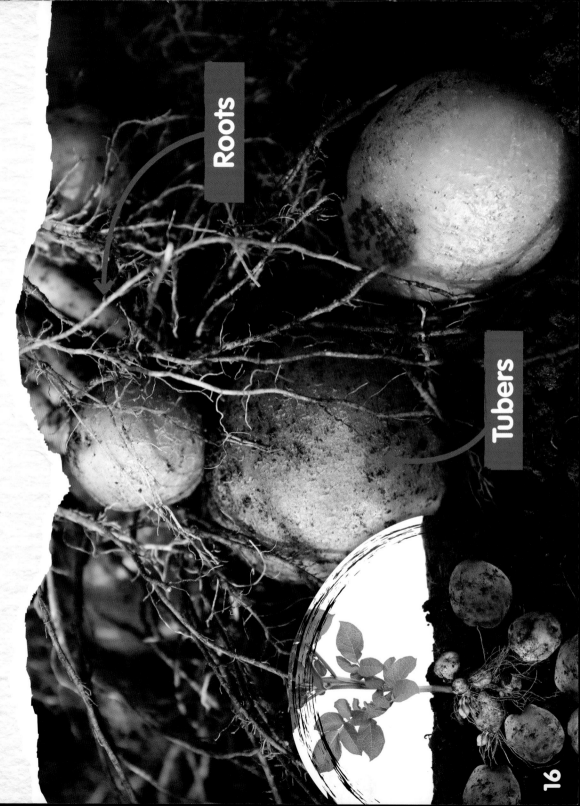

Roots

Tubers

Potatoes come in lots of different types: big, small and lots of different colours. There are even purple potatoes! How many types have you tried?

When they are large enough, they can be harvested and eaten. Yum!

POTATO FACTS

Potatoes are one of the most popular foods in the world! They can be eaten in lots of ways – boiled, mashed, roasted, fried, chips, crisps...

What's your favourite?

Some scientists think that potatoes could be grown in space! Astronauts could grow potatoes on their spacecraft and get lots of nutrients from them when eaten.

Could potatoes be the perfect space food?

WORLD RECORD BREAKERS

World's Heaviest Potato

The heaviest potato in the world weighed almost five kilograms and was grown by Peter Glazebrook in the UK. That's as heavy as a cat! It was shown at a garden show in 2011.

The Most Mash

In 2012, a famous chef and his team cooked up a portion of mashed potato which weighed just over 1,040 kilograms!

That's heavier than a grizzly bear!

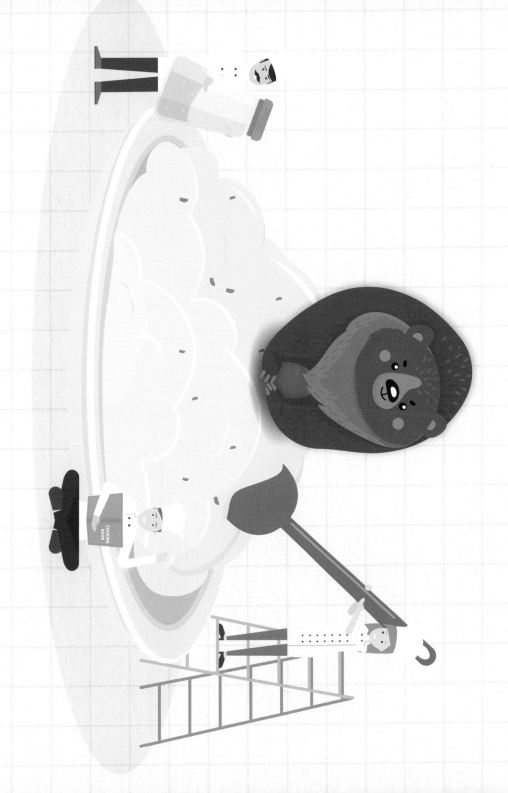

LIFE CYCLE OF A POTATO

2 The sprout grows leaves and a thick stem.

3 The flowers are pollinated and make berries.

LIFE CYCLES

1 The potato sprouts from its eye.

4 New plants can grow from both the seed and the tuber.

GET EXPLORING!

Why not plant a potato of your own and watch the different stages as it grows? Remember – never eat the green parts. Will you grow yours from a tuber or a seed – or both?

23

GLOSSARY

chitting making a potato sprout by putting it in a cool, light place

edible safe to be eaten

energy a type of power, such as light or heat, that can be used to do something

harvested to have picked fully grown crops

nutrients natural things that plants and animals need in order to grow and stay healthy

poisonous dangerous or deadly when eaten

pollinated to have passed on pollen from a plant to another plant of the same kind, so that seeds will be made

rot to break down and decay

INDEX

PHOTO CREDITS

All images are courtesy of Shutterstock.com, unless otherwise specified. With thanks to Getty Images, Thinkstock Photo and iStockphoto. Front cover & 1 – JIANG HONGYAN, Alted Studio. 2 – Titus Group. 3 – Kyselova Inna, Madlen, Fotografiecor.nl. 4 – Gelpi, Samuel Borges Photography, Alla Images. 5 – Madlen. 6 – EVGEIIA. 7 – Brooke Becker. 8 – Krasowit. 9 – Stephen William Robinson. 10 – Elena Maslutkina. 11 – Kazakov Maksim. 12 – SeDmi, Operation Shooting. 13 – Dmitri Malyshev. 14 – oksana2010. 15 – JoannaTkaczuk. 16 – Africa Studio, LilKar. 17 – lucag_g. 18 – Robyn Mackenzie, neil langan. 19 – Flower Studio, mhatzapa. 20 – Fablok, KittyVector. 21 – Inspiring, Tartila. 22 – TwilightArtPictures, N-sky, Yulia 1971, Madlen. 23 – EduardSV.